Discover India
State by State

OFF TO PUNJAB

SONIA MEHTA

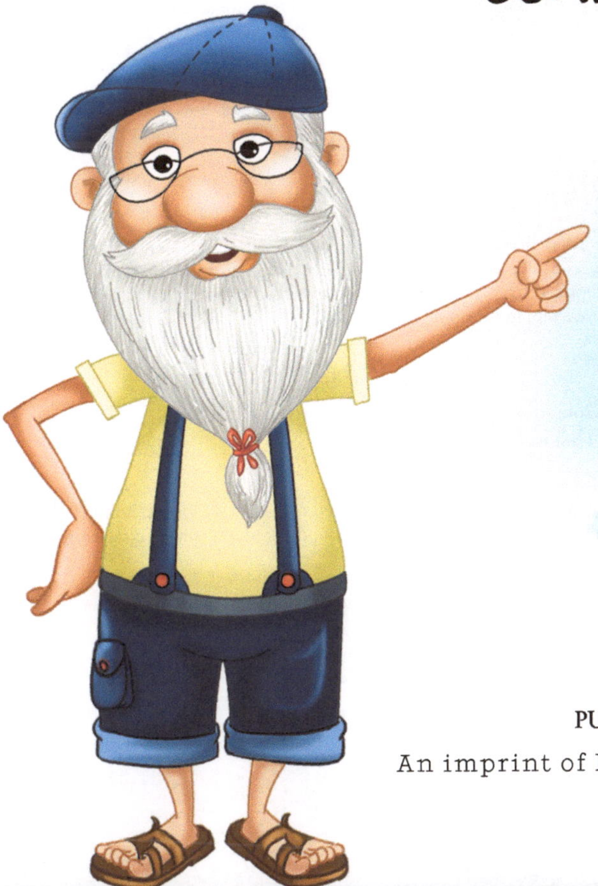

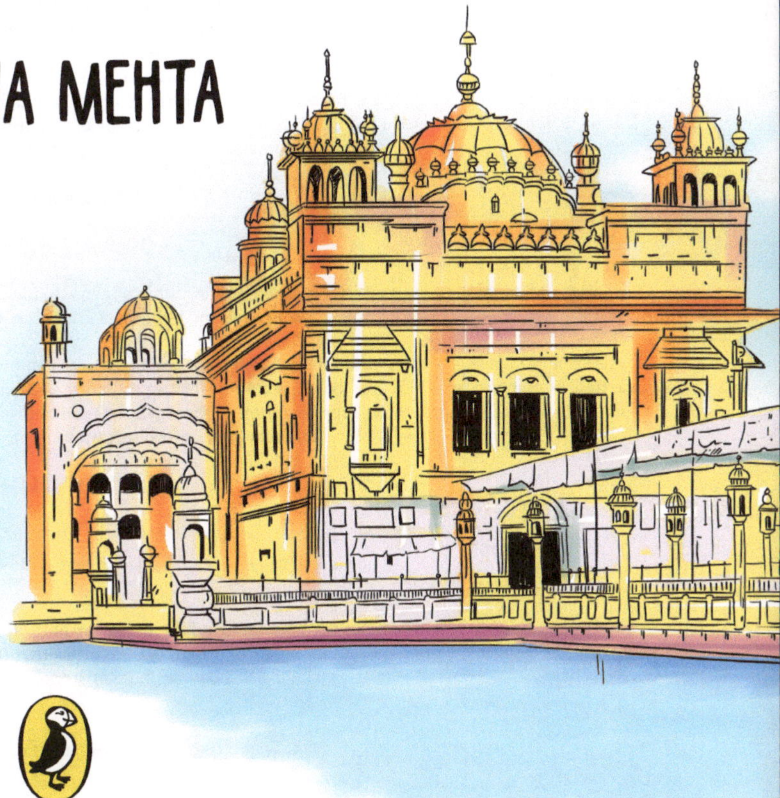

PUFFIN BOOKS
An imprint of Penguin Random House

PUFFIN BOOKS

USA | Canada | UK | Ireland | Australia | New Zealand | India | South Africa | China | Singapore

Puffin Books is part of the Penguin Random House group of companies whose addresses can be found at global.penguinrandomhouse.com

Published by Penguin Random House India Pvt. Ltd
4th Floor, Capital Tower 1, MG Road,
Gurugram 122 002, Haryana, India

First published in Puffin Books by Penguin Random House India 2017

Picture Credits
P 12: Golden Temple, Amritsar (Phuong D. Nguyen/Shutterstock.com), Chandigarh (Ajay Tvm/Shutterstock.com), Patiala (By Journojp (Own work) [CC BY-SA 4.0 (http://creativecommons.org/licenses/by-sa/4.0)], via Wikimedia Commons); P 13: Amritsar (O'SHI/Shutterstock.com); P 20: Rickshaw on Amritsar streets (Phuong D. Nguyen/Shutterstock.com); P 26: A man reading the Adi Granth Sahib (Tukaram.Karve/ Shutterstock.com); P 29: People cooking a feast at the Golden Temple, Amritsar (PRABHAS ROY/Shutterstock.com); P 33: Community kitchen at Golden Temple, Amritsar (Alexander Mazurkevich/Shutterstock.com); P 36: Shri Durgiana Temple (By Guilhem Vellut (originally posted to Flickr as Durgiana Temple) [CC BY-SA 2.0 (http://creativecommons.org/licenses/by-sa/2.0)], via Wikimedia Commons), Silver doors at Shri Durgiana Temple (Diego Delso [GFDL (http://www.gnu.org/copyleft/fdl.html) or CC BY-SA 4.0-3.0-2.5-2.0-1.0 (http://creativecommons.org/ licenses/by-sa/4.0-3.0-2.5-2.0-1.0)], via Wikimedia Commons)

The views and opinions expressed in this book are the author's own and the facts are as reported by her, which have been verified to the extent possible, and the publishers are not in any way liable for the same.

The information in this book is based on research from bona fide sites and published books and is true to the best of the author's knowledge at the time of going to print. The author is not responsible for any further changes or developments occurring post the publication of this book. This series is not a comprehensive representation of the states of India but is intended to give children a flavour of the lifestyles and cultures of different states. All illustrations are artistic representations only.

ISBN 9780143440833

Design and layout by Quadrum Solutions Pvt. Ltd
Printed at Repro India Limited

www.penguin.co.in

Hello Kids!

I'm so happy you are reading this book. India is an incredible country and there are lots of things about it that we never get to hear about.

I discovered India because my father was in the Indian army. He was posted to many places all over India—and we dutifully followed him. Can you imagine that by the time I was in the tenth standard, I had changed nine schools? Of course it was hard making new friends almost every year, but the good part was that I got to live in so many places. Right from Kerala, where I was born, to Kashmir, Jhansi, Shillong, Chandigarh, Goa . . . the list is long.

Every time I go to a new place, I feel amazed at how different each state is from the other—and yet, how similar. Did you know that we can see monuments from the Stone Age right here in India? Or that we have more than twenty official languages, and most Indians know three or four on an average? Or even that some of the world's most amazing scientific marvels were invented in India?

Oh, there are many, many, many fun and fantastic things about the states of India, which we simply must get to know.

So get your backpack ready, get set to meet some new friends and join me on a fun trip as we DISCOVER INDIA, STATE BY STATE.

I hope you enjoy reading this book as much as I have enjoyed writing it. I would love to hear from you. So do write to me at sonia.mehta@quadrumltd.com.

Lots of love,
Sonia Aunty

Mishki and Pushka have come to visit Earth from their home planet, Zoomba. They have never seen such an amazing place. Zoomba doesn't have trees and mountains and rivers like Earth does. But the people look exactly the same. When they come to Earth, they meet a sweet old man whom they call Daadu Dolma. Daadu Dolma shows them all the wonderful places in India and tells Mishki and Pushka all about them.

Mishki and Pushka can't believe what they see. They have seen a lot of Earth, but they have never, ever seen a place like India.

They are off to explore India state by state :)

Mishki

Mishki is a curious little girl. She is always asking loads of questions. On her home planet, she is always getting into trouble for poking her nose into things that are not her business.

Pushka

Pushka is Mishki's brother. He loves adventure. He is always ready to try a new challenge. Whether it's climbing a mountain, or diving into a cold, cold sea, he is up for it.

Daadu Dolma

Daadu Dolma is a wise old man who has lived on Earth longer than the mountains and seas. No one knows quite how old he is, but he certainly has been around. He knows everything about everything.

Mishki and Pushka just can't seem to sit still. They are dying to embark on a trip to one of India's most colourful states.

'Can we leave now?' asks Pushka, jumping up and down.

'Yes, please, Daadu. I have heard so much about Punjab, its dances and its happy-go-lucky culture,' adds Mishki.

'Okay, okay,' says Daadu Dolma, laughing. 'We will leave. You better be prepared for a super trip. Because Punjab is a super place.'

Mishki and Pushka clap their hands. They've been ready for ages. It's what they have been waiting for. They are

OFF TO PUNJAB!!!

A SNEAK PEEK

Land ahoy!

That's a smart question. Punjab literally means 'land of five rivers'. And soon you will know why it's called that.

Daadu, does the word 'Punjab' mean anything?

A BUSY NEIGHBOURHOOD

There is always a lot of action going on around Punjab. That's because the state has so many neighbours. It is wedged between Pakistan, Jammu and Kashmir, Himachal Pradesh, Haryana and Rajasthan. Wow!

To see exactly where Punjab is on the map of India, go to http://www.mapsofindia.com/maps/india/india-political-map.htm

ON THE MAP

ONE, TWO, THREE!

The state of Punjab is divided into three parts. The smallest is the Sivalik range of mountains. Along the foothills of the mountains, there are seasonal streams called *chos*. Lastly, there is the big and fertile plain where farmers work. A large part of Punjab is shaped like a big basin.

The name Punjab comes from the Persian words 'panj' (five) and 'ab' (water).

THE LAND OF FIVE RIVERS

Here's why Punjab is known as the land of five rivers. The Jhelum, Chenab, Ravi, Sutlej and Beas criss-cross the plains of Punjab, making the land absolutely perfect for farming. After India was divided into India and Pakistan, only the Sutlej and Beas remained completely in the state of Punjab. The other rivers flow into other states or into Pakistan.

A LITTLE DRY, A LITTLE WET

Punjab has what is called a continental climate. This means it is kind of dry, except when it is wet. Sounds strange? Well, that's because it has very hot and dry summers. You won't sweat during summer, but you will bake! And winters get very cold indeed! But the state does get a decent amount of rain from July to September—something that farmers wait for anxiously.

A misty morning in Punjab.

Oh, oh! We must look after our trees.

NO FOREST COVER

This is a sad fact! We know that forests do a lot for people as well as for birds and animals. A lot of the forest cover in the Sivalik range has been chopped down over hundreds of years, as people cleared forests and began to farm instead. Naturally, this has impacted the climate. When people realized this, they tried to reforest the hillsides and areas along big roads—which means they planted new trees here.

ANIMAL IMPACT

Since so much forest land was used for farming, wildlife had nowhere to live. There are some animals that made their homes in the agricultural land that is spread across most of Punjab. Rats, squirrels, mice, birds and snakes are some of the species that live happily amidst the fields. Some larger animals like wild boar, leopards, jackals, civets and pangolins continue to live in the Sivalik Hills.

Punjab has many wildlife sanctuaries, where the government tries to protect the animals that continue to make their homes here.

FUN FACTS

State animal
Blackbuck

State tree
Sheesham

State bird
Eastern goshawk (baj)

WHEATY WONDER

A large part of Punjab is devoted to agricultural land. There are many crops that grow here. Did you know that most of India's wheat is grown in Punjab? Just imagine—the chapatti you eat might just be made from the wheat grown here!

Cows resting in wheat fields on a sunny day in Punjab.

Punjab is called the Granary of India or India's Bread Basket.

CROP SHOP

Wheat is not the only thing farmers grow here. Corn, rice, barley, millet—all of these grow aplenty in Punjab. Farmers also grow cash crops like cotton, oilseeds and sugar cane. Many pulses that are grown here find their way into the dals we eat.

Golden wheat fields

The fields of Punjab are such a beautiful sight.

WATER ME WELL

You can imagine how much water is required for agriculture. The government realizes that and has made sure that the land receives plenty of water. This is done by making sure that there are canals that criss-cross the land, carrying river water into every field. There are also many wells, from which people draw water.

MAIZE AMAZE

Which two of these maize stalks are exactly alike? Can you tell?

A   B   C   D

CITY CITY BANG BANG

Punjab has some of India's most vibrant and colourful cities. Let's visit some of them.

CHANDIGARH

The capital of Punjab, this city is often called India's best-planned city. It is actually a Union Territory. It is known for its beautiful gardens and architecture.

Did you know?
Punjab and Haryana share their capital city— Chandigarh.

AMRITSAR

This city is best known for the world-famous Golden Temple. It is said that more people visit this temple than even the Taj Mahal.

BATHINDA

Also known as the City of Lakes, Bathinda is an important railway hub, with trains from many places converging here. It also has one of India's largest cotton and foodgrain markets.

PATIALA

This city is famous in history for the Qila Mubarak (Fort of Good Fortune) and is also well-known for the style of clothing that Punjab is known best for.

I want to visit all these cities!

LUDHIANA

This is a really big city. It sits on the banks of the Sutlej. It is one of North India's most important industrial cities, with lots of factories.

Mishki and Pushka have got to know quite a lot by now. Help them solve this crossword and see how much you remember.

ACROSS

1. The climate of Punjab.

3. The shape of a part of Punjab. Hint: Where you brush your teeth.

4. Punjab's state bird.

5. Villagers draw water from this.

6. A lot of India's _____ comes from Punjab.

7. The colour of the most holy Sikh temple.

8. The state with which Punjab shares a capital.

DOWN

1. The city that is often called India's best-planned city

2. It's a city that is known for its style of clothing, among other things.

3. Punjab is known as India's _____ Basket.

Long, long ago

I see a lot of forts here. What is Punjab's history like?

Punjab has a very eventful history and one that changed the lives of people who lived in this region. Let's start at the beginning.

SO VERY OLD

Like so much of India, the land that is today Punjab has a long and rich history. In the beginning, people from Persia made their way into this region. That's why there is such a Persian influence in the food and habits of the people here. In fact, Alexander the Great, the Greek warrior, invaded India and ruled supreme in the Punjab area for a while.

A statue of Alexander the Great

Mahmud of Ghazni

A BUSY PLACE

The northern part of India in those days was a very busy place, and it was regularly invaded. Punjab was in the middle of it all. The famous dynasty of the Mauryas, led by Chandragupta Maurya, ruled for many years. They were followed by the Kushans and then the Guptas, all of whom conquered and ruled for a while.

MANY INVADERS

Many hundreds of years later, the Huns, a fierce warrior clan, attacked and took control. Then came the Muslim invaders, led by a ruthless king, Mahmud of Ghazni. After several skirmishes and wars over several years, the Mughals overthrew the existing kings and began their long rule.

MUGHAL MANIA

The Mughals were strong kings. They took control of not only Punjab but also almost all of India. King after king, the Mughals strengthened their empire. Babur, Humayun, Akbar, Jehangir, Shah Jahan, Aurangzeb and many others after them made their presence felt. Some of them, like Akbar, were great rulers. They built wonderful mosques, palaces, gardens and forts, many of which we can see even today.

Such a royal entry!

SIKH SALUTE

A hermit called Banda Singh Bahadur became a military leader when he brought together a band of Sikhs. They fought valiantly against the Mughals and the Afghans. Banda Singh Bahadur was defeated and executed, but another great leader was waiting in the wings—Ranjit Singh. He turned the Punjab region into a strong and powerful Sikh kingdom. The provinces of Multan, Kashmir and Peshawar were all part of it—though Multan and Peshawar are now a part of Pakistan.

Sikhism is a religion that was founded by Guru Nanak. The word 'sikh' means 'learner'.

HERE COME THE BRITISH

By this time, Britain and other European countries, like the Netherlands and Portugal, were trying their best to conquer India. The British overcame all these other countries. The British East India Company, which was supposed to be a trading company, became a ruling power that had armies and troops. These troops defeated the Sikhs and made the Punjab region a part of the British colony, like the rest of India.

Banda Singh Bahadur, the brave warrior from Punjab.

FIGHT FOR FREEDOM

The people of India did not like being a British colony at all. The British treated Indian people like second-class citizens. They were not allowed to be in certain places and could not hold particular jobs. Many people from the Punjab region fought for India's freedom.

MASSACRE AT AMRITSAR

A very sad thing happened during this time. A lot of Indian people were protesting and fighting the British. One day, more than 10,000 Indians gathered peacefully at Jallianwala Bagh in Amritsar. A British general named General Dyer ordered his soldiers to fire at these people. There was a terrible stampede. More than 400 people died and over 1200 people were hurt. This did not go down well with the Indians at all. The fight for independence became stronger than ever after this incident.

Did you know?
Some people called General Dyer the Butcher of Amritsar.

FREE AT LAST

Finally, one day in 1947, the British left India and gave back its independence. But there were a lot of arguments between the Hindus and Muslims. It was decided to split India into two countries: India and Pakistan. The Muslims would live in Pakistan. The Hindus would live in India.

Did you know?
People crossed the border on bullock carts or walked for miles.

A TOUGH TIME

Punjab was right in the middle of this partition. The region was split and the western half went to Pakistan, while the eastern half remained in India. It was a very difficult time. Many Hindus who lived in the western part of Punjab were forced to leave their homes and belongings to come to the eastern part. And it was the same for the Muslims who also had to move.

LANGUAGE DIVIDE

Even after Partition, things had not completely settled in Punjab. The Sikhs, who dominated the Punjab region, were keen that their state be a completely Punjabi-speaking one. After much agitation and discussion, in 1966, Punjab was once again split into two states—Punjab and Haryana. Haryana was mostly Hindi speaking, while people in Punjab spoke Punjabi. Some areas in the north became a part of Himachal Pradesh.

नमस्ते   ਸਤ ਸ੍ਰੀ ਅਕਾਲ

Hello in Hindi   *Hello in Punjabi*

A STATE ONLY FOR SIKHS

Although the Sikhs were a majority in Punjab, smaller groups wanted to turn Punjab into Khalistan (which means 'Land of the Pure'). Things were unsettled for a while but soon became peaceful again, and now Punjab is a place that is known for its colour and spirit of joy.

HIDDEN WORDS

How many smaller words can you make from the word given below? Jumble up the the letters and see how many you can make. Mishki has already made one.

CHANDIGARH

HAND
_____   _____   _____

_____   _____   _____

_____   _____   _____

- Hello = Sat sri akaal
- How are you? = Ki haal hai?
- I am fine = Main theek haan
- Thank you = Tu-aada dhanvaad
- Pleased to meet you = Tu-adey nal mil ke badi khushi hoi
- What is your name? = Tu-hada naa ki hai?
- My name is Mishki = Mera naa haga Mishki
- Tell me the way please = Jara rasta dasna
- What? = Ki?
- Where? = Kithey?
- How? = Kiddan?
- When? = Kadon?
- Who? = Kaun?
- Why? = Kyon?

Did you know?
The Punjabi script is called Gurumukhi.

Punjabi is an old, old language. It is influenced quite a lot by Persian, and it can be called an Indo-Aryan language.

LINGO SHINGO

Let's see how much you remember. Without looking at the meanings above, match the English words to their Punjabi translations.

Hello | Thank you | What? | Where? | How are you? | When? | What is your name?

Ki? | Sat sri akaal | Kadon? | Ki haal hai? | Kithey? | Tu-hada naa ki hai? | Tu-aada dhanvaad

A peep into their life

Wow! So much colour. Daadu, it looks like Punjab is a really vibrant place.

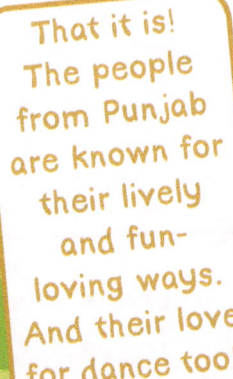

That it is! The people from Punjab are known for their lively and fun-loving ways. And their love for dance too!

LET'S DANCE

Punjabi people love to dance and celebrate life. Songs and dances accompany every occasion, and there are events where everyone takes part—from the oldest granny to the youngest child.

BHANGRA TIME

You must have seen this dance. It used to be performed during the harvest festival, but now people do it at all kinds of celebrations. Dancers perform vigorously to the loud beat of a dhol. When you see a Bhangra performance, you want to dance too!

GO FOR GIDDA

This looks like Bhangra, but it is usually performed by women and is a mix of song and dance. It has a story line and the topics are usually all about family arguments, mother-in-law jokes and other everyday situations. It has an interesting pattern. One of the women will start off with a *boli*, which is when she speaks, and this will be repeated by the other women.

SPOT THE
DIFFERENCE

Can you spot ten differences between the two pictures?

These men are having a blast doing Bhangra!

DHANKARA

This is a dance of celebration. But it is almost like a martial art. Men perform this by holding long staffs or swords. They circle each other and often leap high to loud and lively music. It may look like they are sparring, but they are simply celebrating. They sure do have to be careful though!

I wonder if they get giddy doing this! I would!

KIKLI

This is a simple and fun dance that younger girls perform. They have to do it in pairs or groups of four. They cross their arms, hold hands and use each other for support to spin around at top speed. Must be great fun!

JHUMAR

This is such a happy dance! Performers gather around a drummer to dance. It's usually men who take part. Sometimes, up to three generations get together. So you could see a grandad, a dad and a grandson dancing together at weddings, fairs and festivals.

ODD ONE OUT

In each row, there is one word that doesn't belong. Can you find and circle it?

DANCE   PRANCE   TWIRL   JOG

BHANGRA   KIKLI   DHANKARA   WALTZ

WEDDING   CRICKET MATCH   FESTIVAL   FAIR

DHOL   DRUM   FLUTE   TABLA

SONG   DANCE   SPEECH   MUSICAL PERFORMANCE

READ A POEM, SING A SONG

Punjabi culture is full of poetry, songs and stories. There are ballads of war and love, songs to celebrate festivals and folk music in which everyone enthusiastically joins in. You will find that most of these have either Sikh or Islamic origins.

POETRY FOR THE SOUL

Sheikh Farid

Two great spiritual poets made a deep impact on Punjabi literature. One was the Sufi mystic named Sheikh Farid, who lived hundreds of years ago, and the second was the founder of the Sikh faith, Guru Nanak. Both of these people communicated their messages of peace and love through poetry.

The Adi Granth is the holy book for all Sikh people.

STORIES THAT LASTED

Punjabi literature is just as rich and colourful as the place. One of the first pieces of writing that is recognized as genuine Punjabi literature is *Janam Sakhi*—a biography of Guru Nanak that his best friend and companion, Bhai Bala, wrote. Then there is the world-famous Adi Granth (meaning 'First Book'), which is a collection of poems put together by Guru Arjan.

FAMOUS LOVE STORIES

Just like Romeo and Juliet in the Western world, Punjab has its own famous love story, called Heer Ranjha. It was written by Waris Shah, a renowned poet. There are many Hindi and Punjabi movies that are based on the Heer Ranjha story. Another famous couple in Punjabi literature is Sohni–Mahiwal. People adore these wonderful love stories.

This couple, Heer and Ranjha, are often called India's Romeo and Juliet.

Waris Shah

POETRY PATTERN

Mishki is a great poet herself. Help her find rhyming words for the words given here.

DANCE _____

JUMP _____

TWIRL _____

SWAY _____

SING _____

LEAP _____

FESTIVAL FUN

Aha! Just what everyone in Punjab waits for—a reason to have more fun! There are many festivals that are celebrated with gusto in Punjab, apart from Diwali, Eid and the other Indian festivals. And, of course, there are big Punjabi weddings too.

LOHRI

This is a harvest festival during which people gather around a bonfire on a cold winter night. They dance, eat amazing sweets and sing praises to Dulla Bhatti, one of their heroes.

Dulla Bhatti was like Robin Hood. He was a local king who gave money to the poor by robbing from the rich. He was killed by the Mughals. People admire him even now.

IT'S BAISAKHI!

Baisakhi is a festival where every village in Punjab comes alive. The arrival of this festival means it is time to harvest the rabi crops. Gaily dressed men and women go to the fields. They do the bhangra and gidda to the beat of the dhol. It's also a day to give thanks for a good harvest. There are special Baisakhi fairs too, with food stalls, shops and performances.

GURU NANAK JAYANTI

This is a very special day because it is the birthday of Guru Nanak, who founded the Sikh faith. On this day, there are processions that start at dawn from gurdwaras (Sikh temples). These processions are called *prabhat pheri*. Anyone from any faith is welcome to join. At the end, there is a huge langar. Everyone comes and helps to cook a massive feast.

A langar is a community meal where everyone is welcome to come and eat. There is always enough food.

WEDDING TIME

Punjabi weddings are fun, fun, fun! The wedding goes on for four or five days, and every day there is music, dancing and plenty of food. Women play the dholak and sing songs that tease the bride and groom, and much fun is had by all.

A wedding celebration

HOLI

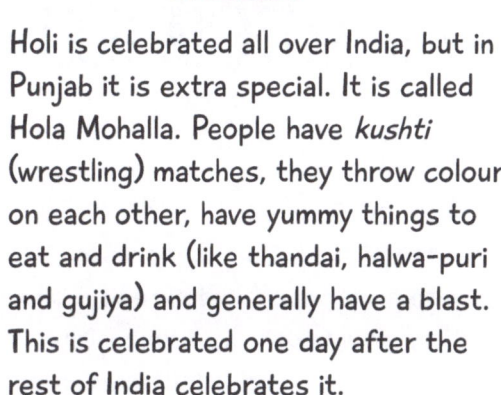

Holi is celebrated all over India, but in Punjab it is extra special. It is called Hola Mohalla. People have *kushti* (wrestling) matches, they throw colour on each other, have yummy things to eat and drink (like thandai, halwa-puri and gujiya) and generally have a blast. This is celebrated one day after the rest of India celebrates it.

Bricks and stones

I would love to visit a typical, old-fashioned Punjabi house. What were those homes like?

I can certainly show you one. Traditional Punjabi houses are found in villages.

Houses had enclosures called *baras*. These were created for cows. Often, guests would be welcomed in this space. In fact, the menfolk sometimes hung out at the baras as well.

THE KUTCHA HOUSE

In Punjab's villages, especially before Independence, a house was built by the people who were going to live in it. So it was a simple structure made of mud, thatch and wood. People would mix mud with wheat chaff and spread it on the ground. Once that dried, they would coat the house with mud that was mixed with cow dung. It may sound yucky, but when dried, cow dung, is cool and clean.

CHANGING WITH THE TIMES

As time passed, newer materials were discovered, and people began to use cement, tiles and metal to build houses. They also began to have more rooms. As people became more aware of sanitation, proper bathrooms with basic plumbing also appeared. Now, only in the very small villages do people live in kutcha houses.

AN OPEN KITCHEN

In traditional houses, there were no properly closed kitchens. Instead, an area that was open to the air and wind was used. It had built-in mud hearths called *chulahs*. Here the women of the house would collectively cook and serve the yummy food they made.

WORD LADDER

Climb the ladder and change **HOUSE** into **SEW**. Follow the clues. Change or drop one letter as you go up the ladder. You might have to rearrange letters too!

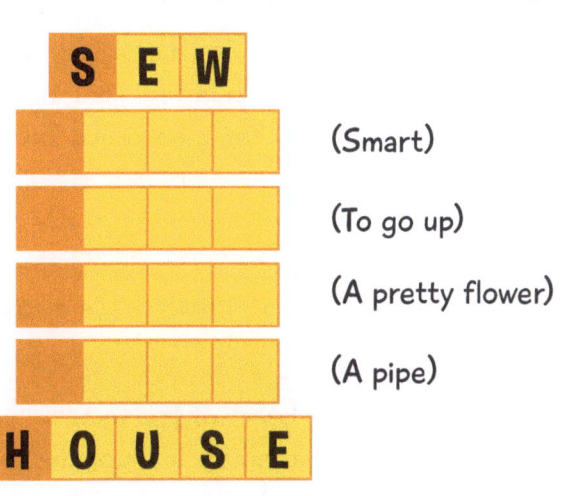

S E W

☐ ☐ ☐ (Smart)

☐ ☐ ☐ (To go up)

☐ ☐ ☐ ☐ (A pretty flower)

☐ ☐ ☐ ☐ (A pipe)

H O U S E

Standing strong

That is coming from Punjab's most famous monument, the Golden Temple. There are many other wonderful monuments we will see too! Come along.

Daadu, what is that golden glow?

GOLDEN FEELINGS

The Golden Temple (Harmandir Sahib) at Amritsar is a beautiful structure that was built by a Sikh guru called Guru Arjan nearly 500 years ago. He also made an entrance on each of the four sides of the temple, to signify that everyone, from all religions and castes, is welcome.

Right in the heart of the temple lies the Adi Granth, the holy book of the Sikhs.

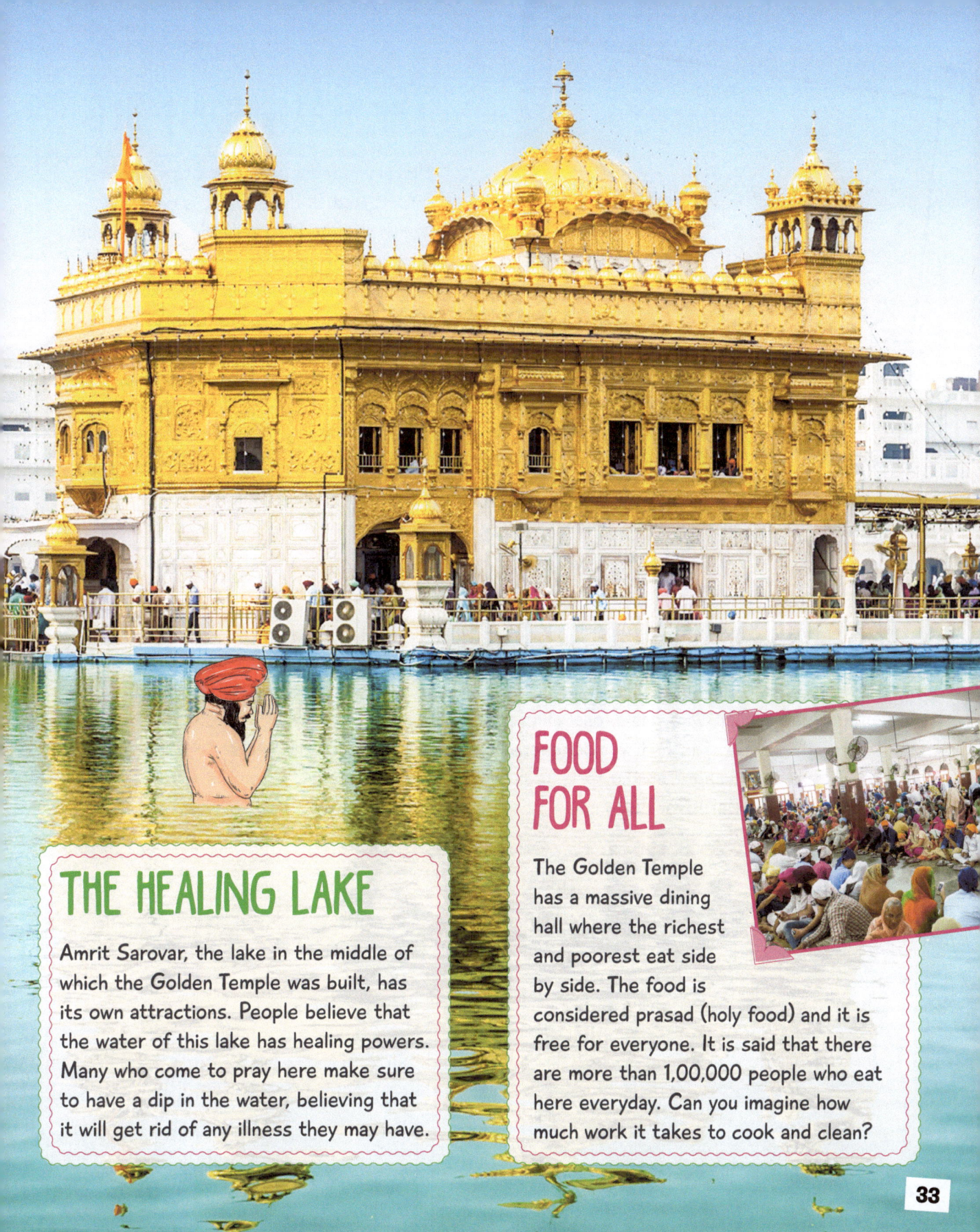

THE HEALING LAKE

Amrit Sarovar, the lake in the middle of which the Golden Temple was built, has its own attractions. People believe that the water of this lake has healing powers. Many who come to pray here make sure to have a dip in the water, believing that it will get rid of any illness they may have.

FOOD FOR ALL

The Golden Temple has a massive dining hall where the richest and poorest eat side by side. The food is considered prasad (holy food) and it is free for everyone. It is said that there are more than 1,00,000 people who eat here everyday. Can you imagine how much work it takes to cook and clean?

THE BATHINDA FORT

History in India is incomplete without a fort. And Bathinda Fort is certainly worth seeing. It's really old and was built hundreds of years ago by the Kushan king Kanishka. It sits in the middle of sand dunes, and the man who built it decided to do something different. He made it look like a ship. The famous warrior queen Razia Sultana was imprisoned here. This fort is called the Qila Mubarak.

Qila Mubarak, Bathinda

Razia Sultana

GOBINDGARH FORT

Gobindgarh Fort was built in Amritsar in the 1760s by Gujjar Singh Bhangi, who was a local chieftain. Initially, it was known as 'Bhangia da qilla'. The fort was conquered by many rulers over the years. When Ranjit Singh captured the fort, he renamed it to Gobindgarh, after the tenth Sikh guru, Guru Gobind Singh.

This is so beautiful.

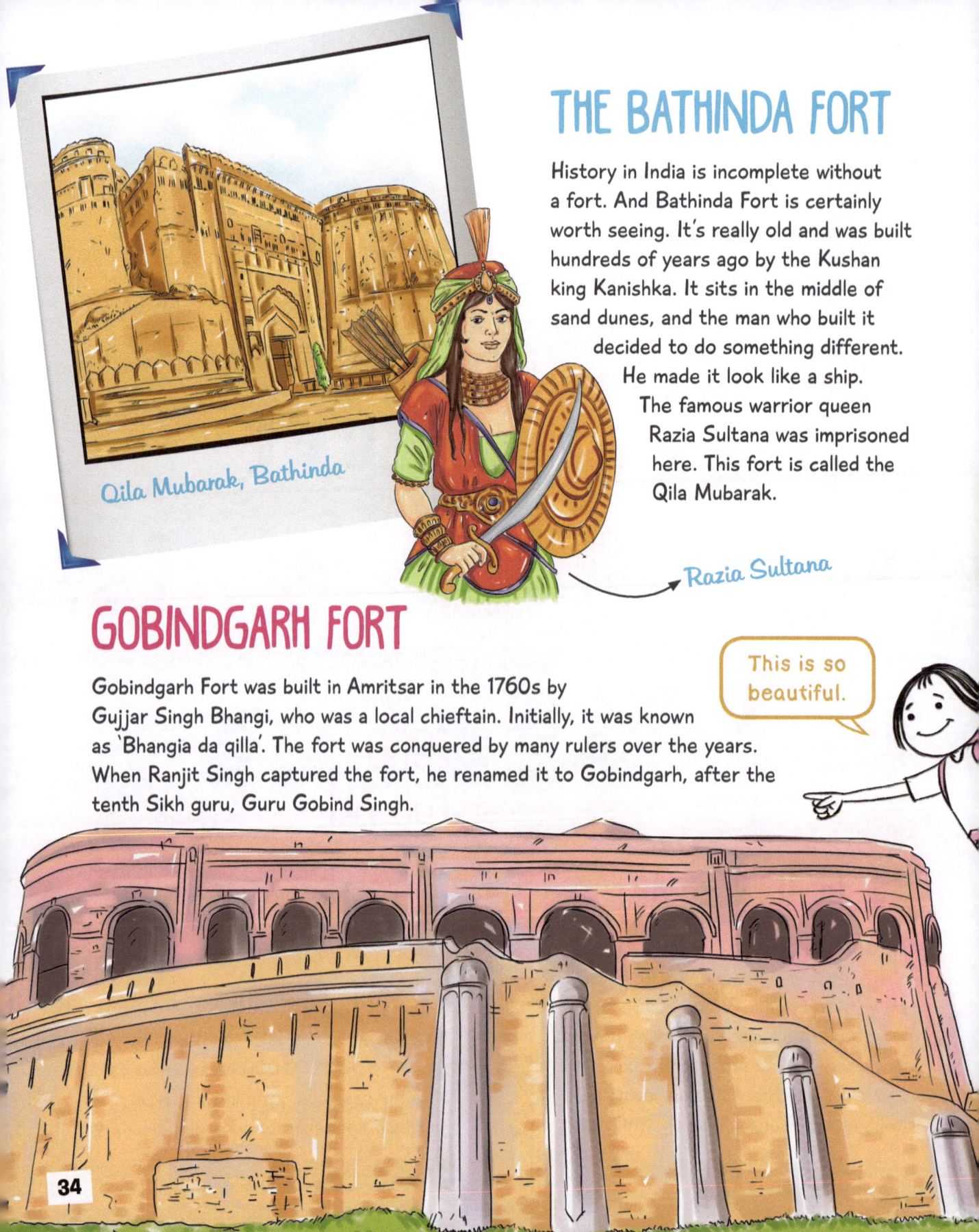

PHILLAUR FORT

This fort was built during the British occupation of India. Ranjit Singh, the man who fought the British so bravely, ordered its construction. But here's something unusual. An Italian engineer supposedly designed the actual construction. Guess what the fort is used for today? The Punjab Police Training Academy uses it to train its students.

CRACK THE CODE

Pushka is climbing Bathinda Fort. But the guard has asked him for the password. Can you help him figure out the password so he can get in?

R = 2	A = 3	Z = 1	I = 4	S = 6	U = 7
L = 8	T = 9	N = 0			

2   3   1   4   3   6   7   8   9   3   0   3

___   ___   ___   ___   ___   ___   ___   ___   ___   ___   ___   ___

SHRI DURGIANA TEMPLE

You have read about the Golden Temple. But did you know that there is a Silver Temple as well? This is a Durga temple that is in the middle of a water tank, just like the Golden Temple. It's called Silver Temple because it has magnificent silver doors. Devotees get together here and sing bhajans at dawn and dusk. How peaceful it must be!

This is so amazing!

THE RAM TIRTH MANDIR

This temple, close to Amritsar, is very special indeed. People believe that the great sage Valmiki wrote the Ramayana near this temple. They also believe that Lord Rama's twin sons, Luv and Kush, were born in this region. No wonder many people visit this temple around the year!

A PALACE OF MIRRORS

A king called Maharaja Narinder Singh came up with a lovely idea. He asked his architects to build a magnificent palace with mirrors and glass. The Sheesh Mahal, as it is called, has paintings of historical stories and legends on its walls and ceilings; coloured glass makes it glow and glitter; and beautiful gardens with fountains make it a wonderful place to stroll around. Must have been amazing to be a maharaja in those days!

GARDEN MAZE

Pushka and Mishki are wandering around in the palace garden. But they have lost their way. Can you help them get out of the maze?

Working hard

People here seem to be having a lot of fun, Daadu! Do they have so much fun working?

The people from Punjab are fun-loving all right. But they are also hardworking, as we will find out.

SERVICE WITH A SMILE

Call centres are places where trained people receive calls from customers and answer all their questions. So when you call someone to complain that your TV isn't working, you are probably calling a call centre.

A lot of people living in this state are part of the service industry. This means that they work in banks, hotels, government offices, courier companies, call centres and so on.

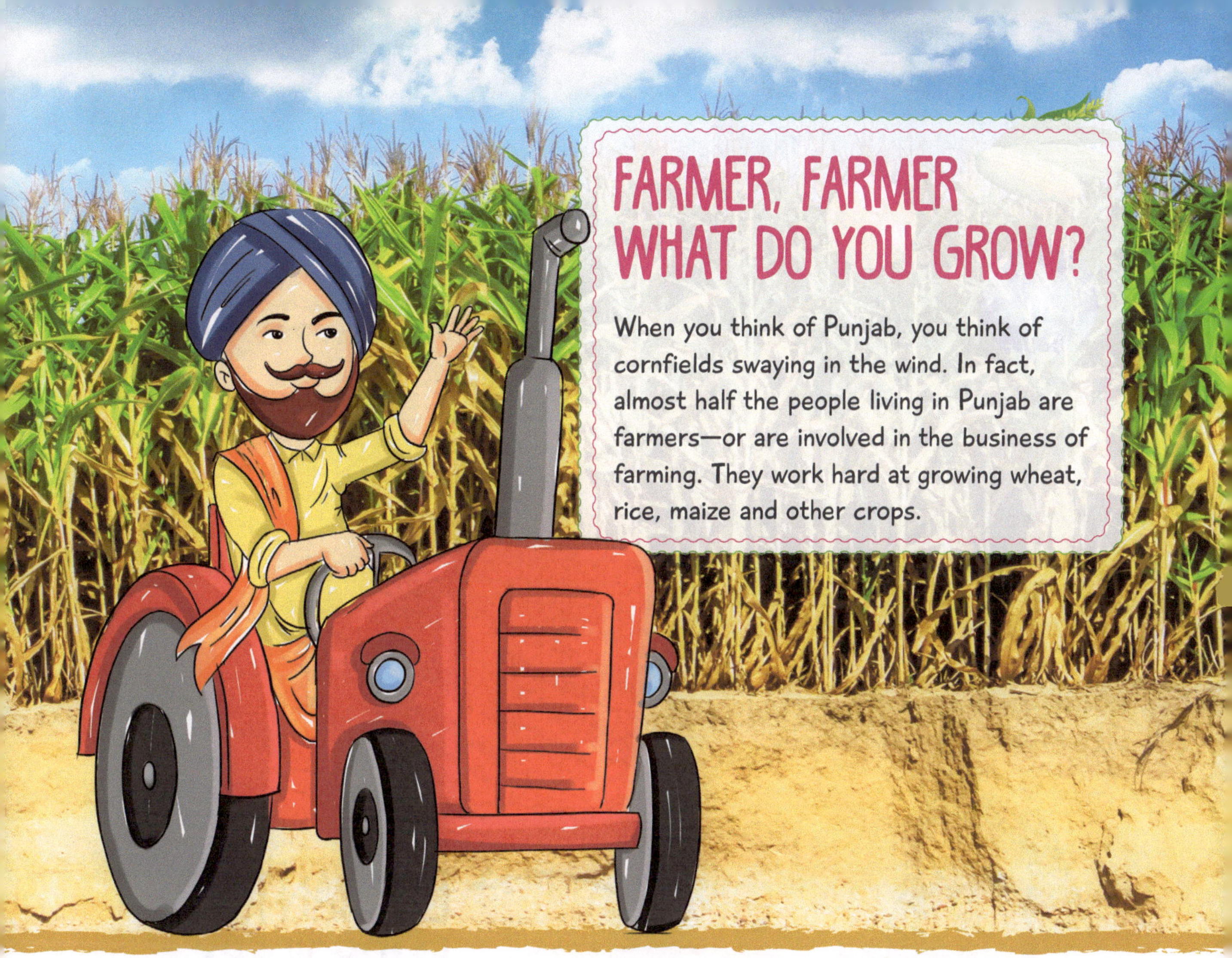

FARMER, FARMER WHAT DO YOU GROW?

When you think of Punjab, you think of cornfields swaying in the wind. In fact, almost half the people living in Punjab are farmers—or are involved in the business of farming. They work hard at growing wheat, rice, maize and other crops.

Punjab is famous for its cotton factories.

FACTORY FEVER

Lots of things are manufactured in Punjab. There are factories for textiles, food and drink, furniture and chemicals. It's a long list. These factories need engineers to run the machines and salespersons to sell the products they make. These industries really keep people busy!

COTTAGE CRAFT

The people of Punjab have always been ever so good with their hands, whether it is weaving, pottery or basket making. Let's see all the amazing things that people in Punjab are so good at making.

BASKET CASE

Basket making is huge in rural Punjab. Earlier, women wove straw baskets to use at home or in the fields. But eventually, the baskets became so popular that people around the world began to buy them. Now, women weave baskets as a profession.

ENCHANTING EMBROIDERY

Phulkari is a kind of embroidery that lots of women do. They have been doing it for centuries. No wonder they are so good at it! Using needle and thread, women stitch detailed designs on shawls, saris and dupattas. The embroidery is done using threads in straight lines.

WOODEN TOYS

It's time for our very own Pinocchios! The wooden toy industry of Punjab is famous. Even though there are fantastic electronic toys today, the simple wooden toys these makers create are magical. It's been an occupation for thousands of years.

Even I want to play with these toys.

BASKET Maze

Mishki has learnt how to weave a basket. Can you go through the weave and see how she should braid the next bamboo strand so she can complete the basket?

Start

Help me get to the finish line!

Finish

Yum yum yum

At last, at last! I am so hungry. I just can't wait any more! Daadu, can we have some yummy Punjabi food?

Yes, for sure. But first, let me tell you all about it. Punjabi food is hearty, healthy and tasty. Some dishes are shared with Pakistani cuisine too!

SARSON DA SAAG AND MAKKI DI ROTI

This is an amazing (and super healthy) winter dish. Sarson da saag is a dish made from mustard greens that are mashed into a yummy paste. It is usually eaten with bread that is made from cornflour, also called makki di roti. Make sure you add a dollop of home-made butter on your rotis! This will keep you full for hours.

RAJMA-CHAWAL

A hot favourite of people in Punjab, this is a yummy gravy made of kidney beans. It's a lovely rich-red colour. People enjoy it with rice and eat it all up till they lick their plates clean. You will too!

MOTHER'S DAL (OR SIMPLY 'MA KI DAL')

This thick, yummy, buttery dal is what many Punjabi moms love making for their kids. It's made of black lentils and cooked with spices for hours, till it becomes rich, creamy and so, so delicious. Make sure you have time for a nap after eating this because it will certainly fill you up.

FRUITY SUDOKU

Pushka is making a fruit salad for dessert. Help him complete the Fruity Sudoku. Draw in the missing fruit in the empty squares. Make sure that every fruit is present in every row, column and mini-square.

AMRITSARI CHANA-KULCHA

No visit to Amritsar is complete without digging into some delicious chana-kulcha. The chana (chick peas) gravy is thick, spicy and delectable. Add to that the soft-as-cloud bread called kulcha and you will be in heaven. A dash of pickle, a dollop of butter and a sprinkling of chopped onion—yes, it's heaven for sure.

You can also have chana with a gigantic type of bread called batura. It can be the size of a football, so you had better be hungry when you decide to eat it.

DEEP PURPLE

Kanji is a deep-purple drink that people in Punjab make in winter. It is made mainly from purple carrots that are available only during the colder months. They are flavoured with mustard and left to marinate for hours in the winter sun. And guess what! Along with being tasty, this drink is super good for health.

LASSI LOVE

Punjabis love lassi. And there sure is plenty available. Lassi, as you probably know, is thick buttermilk. But the lassi you get in Punjab is quite different from anywhere else in India. That's because it is made from the thickest, purest, tastiest milk. There's lots of cream in it. People have it sweet, salty or just plain.

DHABA TRAIL

The best food you get in Punjab is in the dhabas. These are roadside eateries, where people eat quick, inexpensive meals. But the food in dhabas is legendary. So during any visit to Punjab, a dhaba meal is a must.

I want to run my own dhaba. That way I will get all the food I want at all times!

FOODIE SEARCH

Pushka is still hungry. He wants to find all the food he has learnt about. Can you find ten food items in this grid?

K	A	N	J	I	E	R	R	O	T	I	A
D	A	Q	W	L	A	S	S	I	G	F	S
R	I	C	E	G	C	H	A	N	A	A	C
B	A	T	U	R	A	K	S	A	A	G	G
Z	B	U	T	T	E	R	M	K	D	A	L
C	B	H	J	R	A	J	M	A	M	W	F

What to wear?

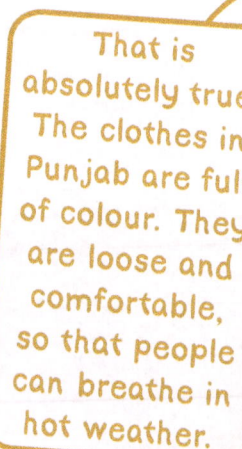

Daadu, the clothes here are so colourful. Even the men seem to wear such bright clothes.

That is absolutely true. The clothes in Punjab are full of colour. They are loose and comfortable, so that people can breathe in hot weather.

THE FAMOUS SALWAAR-KAMEEZ

The clothes worn by women in Punjab haven't changed very much in the last few centuries. Of course, trends have changed, as have some details. But the main outfit is very much the same—a kurta or loose top, which is the kameez, is worn over a pair of baggy trousers, which are called the salwaar. Simply called salwaar kameez, it's now so popular that women all over the world wear it.

The Patiala salwaar is extra loose and billowy, and it needs yards of material.

DUPATTA DELIGHT

The dupatta makes this simple outfit come to life. Women wear elaborate dupattas that are embroidered with intricate patterns in brilliant colours. They cover their heads with it.

PARANDA

Lots of the women here have long hair, which they sometimes plait. Hanging from the ends of these plaits are decorated tassels in bright colours. When these women walk, the tassels swing from side to side.

GHAGHRA GUNG-HO

Before the salwaar became common, women wore a loose skirt called a ghaghra along with the kurta or kameez. Even today, many older women prefer this style.

Kurta

Lungi

RIOT OF COLOUR

The men are no less colourful than the women. The traditional Sikh outfit for men is a kurta and a lungi, but they are not in boring browns and greys. You will find them in vibrant yellows, reds and pinks. This magnificent ensemble is crowned with a colourful turban.

How cool is my turban!

TURBAN TOPPER

Some Sikh men choose to keep their hair very long. In fact, in the Sikh tradition, it is common for men and women to never cut their hair. Men usually wear turbans. This turban is called a *dastar* and is considered a holy gift from the gurus. In the past, turbans used to be up to thirty feet long, but now a turban is usually five feet long. Tying it is a skilful job, and there is quite a science behind it. Today's youngsters wear turbans with modern clothes.

The dastar's baby brother is called a patka. That is the mini-turban little boys wear.

Jhumkas

Sarpesh

BLING FOR ALL

Here's something delightful. In Punjab, there is special jewellery for men and women. During festivals and wedding celebrations, people are dressed to the hilt. Men wear earrings, rings and magnificent ornaments on their turbans. This embellishment is called a *sarpesh*. Women wear elaborate bangles, earrings, toe-rings and necklaces. The *jhumkas* found here are very popular with young girls.

SHOE STYLE

There is a particular style of footwear that both men and women are fond of. It is from this region but is hugely popular all over the world—the Punjabi *jutti*. The tips of these flat shoes are pointed and curl upwards. There are many styles, and some of them have intricate embroidery on them too. Wow!

I would love to own a pair of juttis.

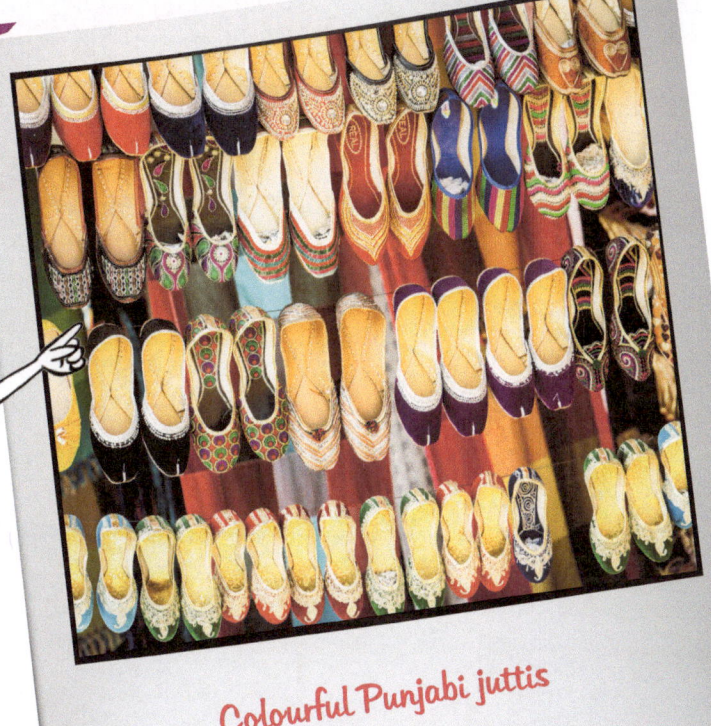

Colourful Punjabi juttis

JUTTI JOY

What a lot of juttis to choose from! Can you find ten differences in these two pictures?

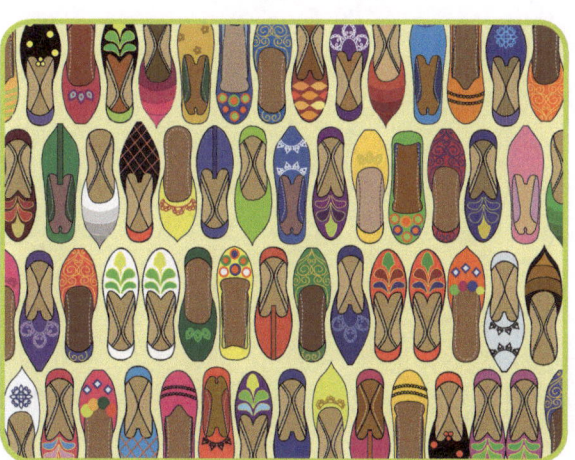

Autograph, please?

Daadu, my autograph book is ready. Who are we meeting today?

There are some really wise and great people in Punjab. There are many sportspersons and Indian soldiers too! Oh, and many, many people from Punjab made it big in Hindi films. Let's meet some of them.

MAHARAJA RANJIT SINGH

He was the leader and founder of the Sikh Empire. He fought the British bravely. This is why he was called Sher-e-Punjab or Lion of Punjab.

SADA KAUR

She was a great military strategist, and was the mother-in-law of Ranjit Singh. She fought and led armies in war, discussed strategies and settlements, and partnered Ranjit Singh during all his brave attempts.

BULLEH SHAH

He was a great poet and philosopher. His poetry revolved around the turbulence the world and his country faced, and his search for God through it all.

SHAHEED BHAGAT SINGH

He was a revolutionary who fought hard against the British. Eventually, he was executed. He is known as a martyr who gave his life for India's freedom. That is why he is called Shaheed Bhagat Singh, as 'shaheed' means 'martyr'.

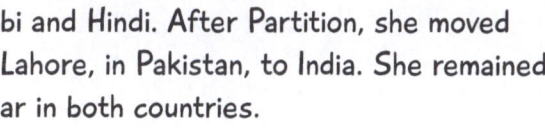

AMRITA PRITAM

She was a poet and writer, who wrote in both Punjabi and Hindi. After Partition, she moved from Lahore, in Pakistan, to India. She remained popular in both countries.

RAJ KAPOOR

When you think of an actor from Punjab, Raj Kapoor comes to mind. He is known as India's greatest showman. Many of his family members are also a part of the film industry.

DARA SINGH

He was a great wrestler who won many titles around the world. He became an actor and played many characters, including Hanuman in the TV series *Ramayana*.

MILKHA SINGH

He is a great athlete and was called the Flying Sikh, due to his amazing speed. He represented India at the Olympics. He also won many medals in the Commonwealth Games.

MANJIT BAWA

He was a famous artist and painter whose works are very valuable. He is renowned for his use of colour.

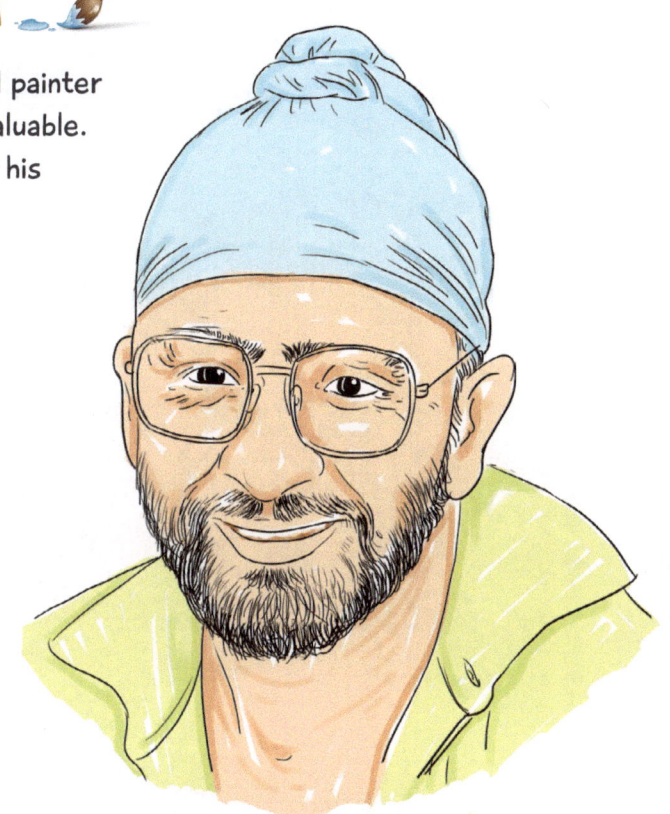

BISHAN SINGH BEDI

He is a great cricketer who is now retired. He was a spin bowler and played many Test matches for India.

MATCH THEM RIGHT

Math the people for what they were known for.

| Actor | Freedom Fighter | Cricketer | Poet |

| Amrita Pritam | Shaheed Bhagat Singh | Bishan Singh Bedi | Raj Kapoor |

Once upon a time . . .

Oh yaaay! Time for a story. I'm sure an interesting place like Punjab has lots of stories.

It does! And I'm going to tell you one about a princess.

SALTY LOVE

There once was a king called Kushal Singh, who ruled over a small kingdom in the dusty heartland of Punjab. He had three daughters whom he loved very much. But he wanted to know how much they loved him.

One day, he put a question to them. 'Tell me, how much do you love me?' he asked. The three princesses gathered around him. The two older daughters were clever. But the youngest, whose name was Amrat, was a simple girl.

'I love you as much as all the gold there is in the world,' said the oldest daughter. The king was pleased with her answer. He gave her a trunk full of gold.

'I love you as much as all the diamonds there are in the world,' the second princess said.

The king was pleased with her answer too. He gave her a trunk full of glittering diamonds.

Finally, it was Amrat's turn. She had been thinking hard.

'Abbu,' she said, 'I love you as much as I love the salt in my food.' The king went purple with anger.

'You ungrateful girl!' he thundered. 'Get out of my sight!'

Poor Amrat was banished from the kingdom. She wandered for days, from village to village. One day, as she was sitting by a stream, a handsome man came galloping up to give his horse some water. He took one look at Amrat and fell in love with her, for she was very beautiful indeed.

When he heard her story, he asked her to come with him to his home. To Amrat's great surprise, he was Prince Shamsher, ruler of a neighbouring kingdom.

'We will invite your father for a meal,' he told her.

Prince Shamsher sent a messenger to King Kushal Singh, inviting him for a feast. The king was pleased.

Prince Shamsher will be the perfect match for my eldest daughter, the king thought. He was even happier when he saw the magnificent feast the prince had arranged.

When the king sat down to eat, he discovered that there was no salt in any of the food. He ate dish after dish but, much to his disgust, every dish was saltless.

'What sort of insult is this?' he roared. 'How dare you serve me saltless food?' The king was about to stomp away angrily, when Prince Shamsher's words stopped him.

'I thought you sent Princess Amrat away because she loved you as much as she loved salt. Now do you see how precious salt is?' Prince Shamsher said, tugging on Amrat's arm to coax her away from her hiding spot behind a pillar, where she had been listening to everything.

King Kushal Singh realized his mistake. He held his arms out and said to Amrat, 'I am sorry, my child. This young man has shown me how wrong I was.'

Prince Shamsher and Princess Amrat were married in a grand ceremony. And you can be sure that there was plenty of salt in the wedding feast.

TRAVEL DIARY

Have you enjoyed this trip to Punjab with your friends Mishki and Pushka—and, of course, with Daadu Dolma?

Now you can make your own Punjab diary. And if you ever visit Punjab, make sure you take pictures and put them in the photo box.

The first place I would visit in Punjab:

_____

If I were a farmer, I would grow:

_____

The one dish I am definitely going to eat:

_____

The monument I think is the most interesting:

_____

The one famous person from Punjab I would love to meet:

_____

If I lived in Punjab, I would be a:

_____

The festival from Punjab that I think is the most fun:

_____

The five words that I think describe Punjab the best are:

_____

_____

_____

_____

_____

My Punjab memories:

ANSWERS

page 11 MAZE AMAZE
A and C are exactly alike.

page 13 CROSSWORD TIME
Across: 1. continental   3. basin   4. baj
5. well   6. wheat   7. golden   8. Haryana

Down: 1. Chandigarh   2. Patiala   3. Bread

page 19 HIDDEN WORDS
HAND, DIG, AND, AN, DIN, RIG, CAR, HIGH, CAN, HIND, RIND, GRAND

page 21 LINGO SHINGO
Hello—Sat sri akal; Thank you—Tu-aada dhanvaad;
What?—Ki?; Where?—Kithey?; How are you?—Ki haal hai?;
When?—Kadon; What is your name?—Tu-hada naa ki hai?

page 23 SPOT THE DIFFERENCE

page 25 ODD ONE OUT
JOG, WALTZ, CRICKET MATCH
FLUTE, SPEECH

page 27 POETRY PATTERN
Prance, Swirl, Ring, Thump, Day, Heap

page 31 WORD LADDER

S	E	W
W	I	S	E
R	I	S	E
R	O	S	E
H	O	S	E
H	O	U	S	E

page 35 CRACK THE CODE
RAZIA SULTANA

page 37 GARDEN MAZE

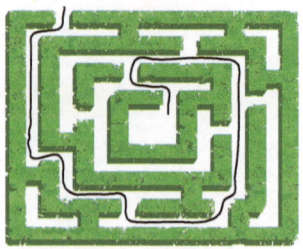

page 41 BASKET MAZE
Start
Finish

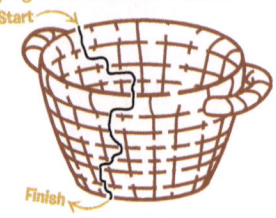

page 43 FRUIT SUDOKU

page 45 FOODIE SEARCH

K	A	N	J	I	E	R	R	O	T	I	A
D	A	Q	W	L	A	S	S	I	G	F	S
R	I	C	E	G	C	H	A	N	A	A	C
B	A	T	U	R	A	K	S	A	A	G	G
Z	B	U	T	T	E	R	M	K	D	A	L
C	B	H	J	R	A	J	M	A	M	W	F

page 49 JUTTI JOY

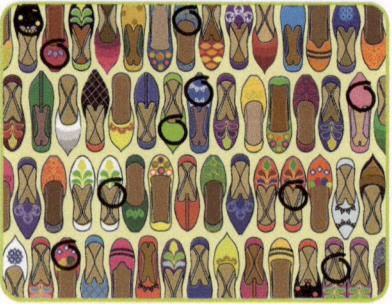

page 53 MATCH THEM RIGHT
Amrita Pritam—Poet; Shaheed Bhagat Singh—Freedom Fighter; Bishan Singh Bedi—Cricketer; Raj Kapoor—Actor